# A Painful History of Crime

# Crime Through Time

John Townsend

# www.raintreepublishers.co.uk

Visit our website to find out more information about **Raintree** books.

To order:
- ☎ Phone 44 (0) 1865 888113
- 🖹 Send a fax to 44 (0) 1865 314091
- 💻 Visit the Raintree bookshop at **www.raintreepublishers.co.uk** to browse our catalogue and order online.

First published in Great Britain by Raintree, Halley Court, Jordan Hill, Oxford OX2 8EJ, part of Harcourt Education.
Raintree is a registered trademark of Harcourt Education Ltd.

© Harcourt Education Ltd 2005
The moral right of the proprietor has been asserted.

Editorial: Melanie Copland
and Kate Buckingham
Design: Lucy Owen
and Bridge Creative Services Ltd
Picture Research: Hannah Taylor
and Ginny Stroud-Lewis
Production: Duncan Gilbert

Originated by Chroma Graphics (Overseas) Pte. Ltd
Printed and bound in China by South China Printing Company

ISBN 1 844 21391 9
09 08 07 06 05
10 9 8 7 6 5 4 3 2 1

**British Library Cataloguing in Publication Data**
Townsend, John
Crime through time – (A Painful History of Crime)
364.9
A full catalogue record for this book is available from the British Library.

**Acknowledgements**
Alamy Images 30-31 (David Crausby), Corbis pp 33b; 1, 4, 9b, 39, 40 (Royalty Free), 10-11, 26t, 33t, 34 (Bettmann), 28-29 (Charles Mann), 8 (Craig Aurness), 23 (David Woods), 7 (George D. Lepp), 20 (Helen King), 42 (Jutta Klee), 29 (K M Westermann), 35 (Reuters), 27 (Sygma), Getty Images pp 5 (The Image Bank), 5t, 11, 12-13, 12, 16-17, 16, 31, 32, 37 (Hulton Archives), 5b, 36 (Time & Life Pictures), Harcourt Education Ltd pp 22, 26b (Ginny Stroud-Lewis), 24 (Tudor Photography), Mary Evans Picture Library pp 5m, 15, 18, 19, 21, 25, Science Photo Library pp 38-39 (Andrew Syred), 41 (TEK Image), The Kobal Collection pp 43; 13, 20-21 (20th Century Fox), 9t (MGM), 6-7 (Paramount/Dreamworks /Douglas Curran), 14 (Walt Disney Pictures/Elliott Marks).

Cover photograph of crowbar reproduced with permission of Alamy Images/ Elmtree Images.

Every effort has been made to contact copyright holders of any material reproduced in this book. Any omissions will be rectified in subsequent printings if notice is given to the publishers.

The paper used to print this book comes from sustainable resources.

# Contents

Any words appearing in the text in bold,
**like this**, are explained in the glossary. You can
also look out for them in the Word bank box at
the bottom of each page.

# Breaking the law

Have you ever committed a crime? You may have broken the law more often than you think! If you chew gum in the street or wink at someone in town, you might be a **criminal**! In some parts of the world, you could be **arrested** for these crimes.

Crime does not mean the same thing in every country. Crimes were different in the past, too. In different times and places, crimes have changed a lot. But many of the reasons people turn to crime in the first place have hardly changed at all.

Through history, people have been arrested for some odd crimes.

*Word bank*   criminal   person who has committed a crime
illegal   against the law

## Telling the truth

Laws tell us what we can and cannot do. A crime is any action or behaviour that is against the law at a particular time or place. A criminal is anyone who breaks the law and commits an **offence**.

For thousands of years, criminals have been punished for their crimes. But the way the courts have dealt with crime has changed a lot over the years. At one time if you told a lie your tongue would be cut off. Today we treat liars a bit differently! After all, there might not be many people around who could still talk!

### Find out later...

Why were some people burnt at the stake?

When were poisoners boiled alive?

When were fingerprints first used to catch criminals?

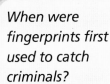

✝ In some US cities (like Ottumwa, Iowa) it was once **illegal** for men to wink at women in the street.

**offence** breaking of the law

# Why crime?

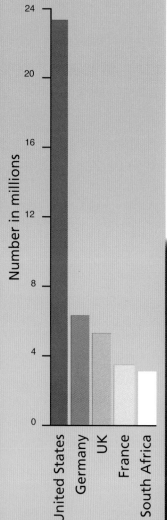

Number of crimes reported in different countries in 2000

**Number in millions** (y-axis: 0, 4, 8, 12, 16, 20, 24)

Countries (x-axis): United States, Germany, UK, France, South Africa

Although some people may not mean to break the law, most criminals know exactly what they are doing. When they set out to commit a crime, they know the risks they are taking. Through history people have committed crimes mainly to get money or property, or to get rid of an enemy. There are still three main types of crime. They are against:

- Property (such as burglary or **vandalism**). Many crimes today involve stealing or damaging something that belongs to other people.
- People (such as murder, assault or armed robbery).
- **Authority** (such as **treason**, protest or **terrorism**).

*Word bank*   **treason**   crime of trying to overthrow the government or authority

As soon as people become criminals, they risk being punished. So why do they commit crimes in the first place? There have always been five main reasons:

- Need – when people are too poor to buy what they need or want.
- Gain – when people steal and sell stolen goods to make money.
- **Impulse** – when people suddenly act without thinking or planning. They may act in anger or fear.
- Influence – when people are affected by drugs, alcohol or bad friends.
- Belief – when people believe the law is wrong and break it to make their point. They believe their crime will change others' minds.

## Road crime

Another main cause of crime today is the car. People often break traffic laws that are meant to protect drivers. Millions of drivers get caught each year for driving too fast. Speed cameras turn many drivers into criminals in a flash!

Often committing a crime ends in a police chase as the criminals try to make their escape..

terrorism  use of terror to achieve a goal
vandalism  damaging property on purpose

# Ancient times, ancient crimes

Today we have more laws than ever before ... and more criminals. But that is because there are more people on Earth today than ever before. It does not mean people today behave any worse than they used to.

## Early days

Laws were first made and written down by **ancient** civilizations. They were often based on a common sense view of right and wrong. Some people then, and today, believe that laws came from their gods. So if someone broke a law, they made the god unhappy or angry. Punishing the criminal harshly was often thought to please the god.

### China

Some of ancient China's laws were set down over 4,000 years ago. People had to meet each month to hear them.

- Pick-pockets were **branded** on the arms.
- Armed robbery was punished by death.
- Any girl who insulted her parents was strangled. If she hurt them she was cut up into pieces.

A red hot branding iron would mark a criminal for life.

*Word bank*    **ancient**  from a time thousands of years ago
**pharaoh**  ruler of ancient Egypt

# Egypt

In ancient Egypt 4,000 years ago, the country's rulers were seen as gods. These rulers, called **pharaohs,** made the laws and enforced them. They had control over the people and punished them for doing wrong. The worst crime was tomb raiding because the treasures in the tomb were **sacred.** Anyone caught could be drowned, beheaded, burnt alive or thrown to the crocodiles.

Roman criminals were treated harshly, as seen in this image from the 1959 film *Ben Hur.*

The pharaoh's officers would catch the criminals and bring them before the pharaoh. He would decide the punishment in court. For some crimes people were beaten in public. They might even have their nose cut off. So it was wise to obey the law!

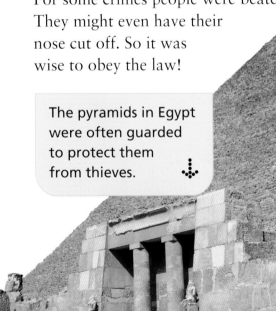

The pyramids in Egypt were often guarded to protect them from thieves.

## Roman times

There was a lot of crime in Rome 2,000 years ago. The **slums** were risky places to go as theft was very common. The Emperor Augustus paid men to patrol the city but they had little effect in the poor areas. Rich people did not worry too much as they rarely visited the slums.

**sacred**   holy and worthy of respect
**slum**   crowded and run-down part of a town

## Hard times

One thousand years ago, people in Europe had to be careful. It was a cruel time, with many laws being made based on religion. Religious leaders were very powerful. It was a crime to disagree with their teaching. Anyone found **guilty** of having other beliefs could be put to death. How could you prove you were not guilty? It would need a "Trial by **ordeal**". You would have to take a test like:

- swallowing poison
- pulling an object from boiling oil
- walking over red-hot metal
- carrying red-hot iron over a distance

Guess what? If you died or got hurt, you were guilty because God had not protected you.

### The Middle Ages

The years from 800 to 1500 are now called The **Middle Ages**. It was a time when many punishments were used for people who broke laws or upset religious leaders. Across Europe and Arab countries, people believed strongly in different religions.

A painting of a woman on a ducking stool, which was used as a punishment for many crimes.

*Word bank*   **Middle Ages**   period of European history from about 800 to about 1500

## The crime of speaking

Women in the Middle Ages were not treated fairly. Laws in Europe made them guilty of crimes which do not exist today. One of these crimes was nagging! A nagging wife could be punished for the crime of being a **scold**. A punishment for this was to be ducked in the local river on a ducking stool. People would come and cheer each time the woman went under the water.

Another punishment for nagging too much was to wear the Scold's Bridle. This was a metal mask full of sharp spikes that poked inside the woman's mouth. If she tried to speak ... ouch!

### Knife crime

Violent crime was a problem in some cities of Europe in the Middle Ages. This was because most people carried knives. Although these were just everyday tools, they became weapons when fights broke out. **Taverns** often saw violent fights.

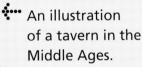
An illustration of a tavern in the Middle Ages.

scold    someone who keeps complaining and nagging
tavern    "ale house" where alcoholic drinks are sold and drunk

## Witches

In the 1400s many people thought the world's problems were caused by the devil. They believed the devil had helpers on Earth, like witches, to carry out his evil work. In 1484, the **pope** blamed witches for casting evil spells. This began the big European Witch Hunt, which lasted for nearly 200 years.

The crime of being a witch was punished by being burnt alive. Anyone who was thought to be a witch was **tortured** first. Many people admitted being witches just to stop the pain of torture. Witches were not just old women dressed in black. Anyone who appeared "different" or odd could be **arrested** and burnt.

### Burning

No one really knows how many people were put to death across Europe from 1450 to 1750 for the crime of being a witch. Historians think that perhaps 40,000 people were burnt alive after being **accused** of witchcraft. Most of those had probably done very little wrong at all.

Being burnt at the stake was a common punishment for being a witch.

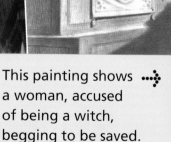

This painting shows a woman, accused of being a witch, begging to be saved.

**Word bank**   **pope**  head of the Roman Catholic church
**smallpox**  deadly fever and rash caused by a virus

## Salem witches

In 1692 witch-hunting caused trouble in America. In Salem, New England, two women had a mystery illness. Their doctor said witches must have made them ill. This started a panic. After an outbreak of **smallpox**, some people thought the devil was at work. Salem people lived in fear. The crime of witchcraft was blamed for these events. It had to be stamped out.

A few local girls became ill and cried out people's names. Anyone whose name was called by a sick person was arrested. Over 150 men and women from around Salem were put in prison. Trials followed which sent people to their deaths.

Many people were arrested and taken away in Salem. This picture is from the 1996 movie *The Crucible*.

### The crime of 1692

The witch trials at Salem led to the hanging of nineteen men and women. An 80-year-old man was crushed to death. He was made to **confess** ... by being pressed under a heavy weight. Seventeen other **suspects** died in prison.

**torture** causing someone great pain especially to punish or to obtain a confession

# Thieves

Taking people's property has always been a common crime. Thieves and robbers have stolen because of need, greed, **revenge** or just for fun.

MARY FRITH,
ALSO CALLED
MOLL CUTPURSE
DIED 1659,
LONDON - AGED 74.

A FRIEND OF
HIGHWAYMEN
AND A RECEIVER OF
STOLEN GOODS.

Mary Frith was a thief, and was sent to Newgate Prison in the 1600s.

An image from the 2003 movie *The Pirates of the Caribbean.*

## Pirates

Around the same time that people were being **arrested** for witchcraft, crimes at sea were growing. Pirates were the robbers of the seas. They attacked ships and stole their treasures.

A pirate ship called *The Whydah* sank off New England, United States in 1717. One of its dreaded pirates was called Quintor. He and five others escaped the sinking ship but were caught later. They were hanged for the crime of **piracy**. People cheered as their bodies swung from the ropes around their necks.

*Word bank*    flintlock musket   gun with a flint making a spark to fire the gunpowder

## Highwaymen

In the 1700s, in both Europe and the United States, roads were just rough tracks. Most people travelled between towns by horse or on foot, but wealthy people used wagons or carriages. These were quite slow and the wheels often got stuck in the rough ground. So rich people, in the middle of nowhere, on tricky roads meant .... CRIME!

Robbers called highwaymen or "road agents" would hold up the carriages and rob the people inside. Some of these robbers were just violent thieves. Others dressed smartly, were very polite and became known as "gentlemen robbers".

This painting shows highwaymen in action. ⁝

### The start of gun-crime

Although the first guns were made in the 1400s, it was in 1700s that American gun makers made guns like the Brown Bess **flintlock musket** for soldiers. It could shoot up to about 80 metres. By the mid 1700s robbers and highwaymen were able to get hold of such guns. This changed the world of crime forever.

piracy   robbery on the high seas
revenge   get even for a wrong done

## Poachers and smugglers

**Poaching** has been a crime for hundreds of years. By the 1700s it became more common in the UK when farm workers were so poor. Many of them turned to poaching to survive. Rich land owners tried to stop these poachers taking animals from their land. They set man-traps to catch poachers, to break their legs or even to kill them.

The law made poaching a serious crime. Between 1750 and 1820, many poachers were hanged. From 1816, anyone caught poaching could be sent across the world to prison in Australia for 14 years. But many people were so hungry they still risked poaching rabbits "for the pot".

### Stealing meat

Poaching means the **illegal** hunting and trapping of deer, hares, pigeons and other animals from private land. For hundreds of years poachers have caught animals to sell on the **black market**. Other people poached animals to provide food for their family (shown in the painting above). Poaching is still a crime today.

*Word bank*   **customs**   office at borders of countries where taxes are paid on imports or exports

## Smuggling

Smuggling is a crime that steals money from governments. It became a big crime in about 1300 when the British government put a **tax** on wool. The wool tax meant anyone who sold wool had to pay part of their profit to the government. Wool was a very important **export** at this time. So some wool sellers smuggled the wool out of the country in boats at night to avoid paying the tax. Then they could avoid **customs** at harbours and ports.

Ever since, criminals have smuggled goods in and out of countries. It is still big crime today.

## Whisky smuggling

The smuggling of whisky was a major crime in the United States in the 1920s. A law banned the buying and selling of alcohol. This law was called prohibition. No bars were allowed to sell whisky – so smugglers made a lot of money by getting whisky and selling it illegally.

A painting showing smugglers coming ashore under cover of darkness.

**export**   goods sent to another country to sell
**poaching**   stealing animals from private land

17

## Breaking in

Breaking into houses to steal money, jewels, paintings or antiques is an old crime. It was once called house-breaking. Today **burglars** are more likely to steal DVD players, TVs and computers.

In fact, the crime of burglary is the **illegal** entry into any building, not just a house. Stealing other people's property by breaking in and carrying it away is sometimes called **larceny**. In the United States, this crime is called grand larceny if the value of the goods stolen is over US$200.

Many house owners today not only fit burglar alarms but also CCTV cameras to keep the burglars away.

### Catching thieves

Although there was no proper police force anywhere in the world in the 1700s, many cities had watchmen to keep a look-out for crime. Some men called themselves "thief-takers" and charged to track down burglars on the prowl at night.

This illustration ⋯⋗ shows house-breakers entering a house during the night.

*Word bank*   **burglar**   someone who breaks into a building or house to steal, especially at night

## A helping hand

In the **Middle Ages** and later, many burglars believed in magic powers.

The "hand of glory" was an old European idea that some burglars tried. They used to cut off the hand of dead criminals who were left hanging on the **gallows**. Then they either made the fat from the hand into a candle or they put a candle in the hand itself. By lighting the candle when breaking into a house at night, the burglar believed the owners of the house would stay fast asleep.

It was probably more likely that the home-owner would faint from the shock of seeing a lighted hand!

Jack Sheppard, ⋯⋰ who lived from 1702–1724.

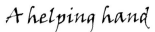

### Famous house-breaker of 1724

**July:** Jack Sheppard, charged with many house burglaries, escaped from Newgate Prison in London. He was later caught and sent back to prison.

**October:** Jack Sheppard made yet another escape from prison.

**November:** Jack Sheppard was caught again.

**December:** Jack Sheppard hanged.

**gallows**   wooden frame from which criminals were hanged
**larceny**   crime of carrying away someone's personal property deliberately

# Bank robbers

Since the first banks were built, thieves have found ways to get in and steal the cash. At some times in some places, bank robberies got out of control. The west of the United States had a crime wave in the mid 1800s. Bank robbers with guns rode into many "wild west" towns – to gallop away with hundreds of dollars.

When gold and silver were found in the mountains of California, Colorado and Montana, more banks had to be built. That was just right for the robbers. Money was there for the taking. Gangs of **outlaws** on horses went from one town to another. No bank was safe.

Bank robbers in the 1939 movie *Jesse James*.

*word bank*    **outlaws**   criminals who lived "outside the law"

## Crime waves

At certain times, bank crime has suddenly grown. Within a few years it can die down again. A sudden crime wave hit Chicago, United States, in the 1920s. The city was in the grip of gangsters. Money problems across the country, easy access to machine guns, and cars for quick get-aways brought gangs of criminals to the streets. Banks were often their target.

Today bank robbery can still be a problem. From 1996 to 2001 bank robberies in US towns increased by over 35 per cent. There were over 8,000 bank robberies in the United States in 2001. Perhaps in the future all banks will have armed guards.

An illustration of robbers holding up a bank in Philadelphia in 1871.

- John Price stole a goose;
- Elizabeth Powley (22 years old) took some bacon, flour and butter from a kitchen;
- Thomas Chaddick raided a kitchen garden for some cucumbers;
- John Wisehammer (15 years old) stole some tobacco powder;
- William Douglas picked a silver watch from a gentleman's pocket.

All were shipped off to prison in Australia from the UK.

Being a pickpocket ···› in the 1700s could get you sent away on a prison ship!

# From need to greed

People were once sent to prison for crimes that they would only have to pay a fine for today. Prisoners could be sent across the world to other countries. The UK sent convicts to the United States in the 1700s – before shipping over 160,000 to Australia from 1788 to 1868. Many of these convicts had committed only minor crimes such as stealing food or clothes for their family. Most people stole because they were hungry and too poor to buy food. They were very different from the full time "professional" thieves who stole out of habit or greed. Today many professional criminals are super-rich.

*Word bank*    **fraud**   cheating people out of money by deceiving them in some way

## Changing times

Much of today's theft is done by full-time thieves. They not only earn their living from crime but many make huge sums of money. They see crime as the way to keep them in a rich lifestyle. But many lose it all when they get caught!

### Crimes reported in 2000

|  | Burglaries | Car thefts |
|---|---|---|
| United States | 2,099,700 | 1,147,300 |
| United Kingdom | 836,027 | 338,796 |
| Australia | 436,865 | 139,094 |

Today's prisons are full of criminals who have been involved in organized crime. This often involves large scale:

- Car theft
- **Fraud**
- **Cyber crime**
- Art theft
- **Identity theft**

Such crimes are a long way from petty theft of the past. Crime now may be bigger and better organized – but so are the police. Getting caught is more likely today than 100 years ago!

Car theft is a major crime today.

**identity theft**   stealing people's personal details and pretending to be them

# Killers

## Did you know?

Today in the USA, there are three types of murder according to the law:

- First-degree murder – where the killer sets out to murder on purpose.
- Second-degree murder – where the killer acts in the heat of the moment.
- Third-degree murder (also known as manslaughter) - where someone kills by mistake, like in a car crash.

Murder is a crime that has been committed through history, all over the world. For much of that time, being convicted of murder has carried the **death penalty**. In some countries it still does. The killing of another human being on purpose is also called **homicide**.

## Why kill?

People have killed for many reasons. They may have killed to:

- steal someone's property
- stop someone talking or telling secrets
- make life better or safer for themselves or others
- get **revenge**
- feel powerful.

Since Greek and Roman times, a common murder weapon has been quick and silent: Poison.

Poison – the quick and silent killer.

*Word bank*    evidence   material presented to a court to help find the truth in a crime

# Poisoners

Poison is used in only about 3 per cent of murders today. In the past it was used a lot. Murderers could once get poison easily or make some from plants. It was then a matter of slipping the poison into someone's food or drink ... and escaping. Often victims would appear to die of an illness and no one would know they had been killed.

Today it is not so easy to get away with poisoning. Modern science can show what type of poison was used, how much and when it was given. Small traces of the poison can often be found on the murderer and used as **evidence** in court.

## Another for the pot

At one time in Europe, any poisoner could be boiled alive. Margaret Davy was a servant who was blamed for poisoning the family she worked for in the UK. In 1542 she was lowered into boiling water several times until she was dead. Five years later the law changed and the boiling of poisoners stopped.

An illustration of two men being boiled alive and showered with boiling water.

## Serial killers

All through history some killers have struck for no apparent reason. Sometimes they killed again and again before being caught. The term "serial killer" was first used for such criminals by the **FBI** in the 1970s. Yet they have been around for hundreds of years. These were just three of them:

- In the 1400s, one of the richest men in France was Gille de Rais. He murdered at least 100 children.
- Elizabeth Bathory lived in Hungary. She was **arrested** in 1610 and charged with killing as many as 600 young girls.
- Joseph Vacher was executed in France in 1898 after **confessing** to killing 11 women and children.

### Chicago killer

Over 100 years ago Herman Mudgett (above) was a killer in Chicago, United States. He pretended to be a doctor and gassed his patients. During a fire, fireman found their bodies. Between 20 and 100 people had been killed – maybe as many as 200. Mudgett confessed to 28 murders. He was hanged in 1896.

Serial killers have used a variety of weapons to kill their victims.

**Word bank**    convicted    proved to be guilty

## The killing habit

A serial killer is someone who commits three or more murders over a long period. In between their crimes they can appear to be quite normal and seem very pleasant. Many serial killers kill to get power over others. Some have even enjoyed teasing the police by sending them notes or taped messages.

## Mystery

Murders are often full of mystery. Apart from having no obvious reason for killing, some murderers in the past were never discovered. In fact, with modern science, it has recently been possible to solve murders from long ago. See how on page 41.

‡∙∙∙ Harold Shipman, after he was arrested.

### 21st century

In 2000, Dr Harold Shipman was **convicted** of murdering 15 patients. He is now believed to have killed hundreds more, making him the worst serial killer in British history. He was sent to prison, where he hanged himself in 2004.

---

**FBI** United States' Federal Bureau of Investigation, which investigates serious crime

## Murder

Killing another person has not always been seen as murder. So when can someone who kills another human not be **accused** of murder?

- Soldiers who kill enemy soldiers in times of war.
- Victims of attack who kill an attacker in self-defence.
- Someone with mental illness who kills in a confused state of mind.

It is murder to kill another human even to save yourself from death. Shipwrecked sailors were adrift off the coast of South Africa in the 1880s. Two of the sailors killed a sick cabin boy so they could eat him to survive. They were later sent to prison in England for murder.

Today most murders in the United States are carried out using guns.

## Rising crime?

The United States has more people than any other country, after China and India. With so many people, it is not surprising the United States has some of the highest murder figures. On average, in the 21st century, someone in the United States is murdered every 32 minutes! The most common murder weapons are guns.

Although the number of people in the country keeps rising, at the start of the 21st century, the number of crimes reported in the United States has gone down. That's the good news. The bad news was that the crimes burglary, car theft, and murder started increasing again in 2001–2003.

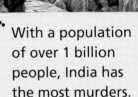

With a population of over 1 billion people, India has the most murders.

### Countries with the most murders

The country with the most murders in 1999 was India with 37,170 killings!

Russia: 28,904 (2000)

Colombia: 26,539 (2000)

South Africa: 21,995 (2000)

Mexico: 13,829 (2000)

# Criminals with a mission

## Keep quiet

In the 1400s and 1500s, kings and queens in Europe often believed God wanted them to rule. So anyone who disagreed with a king or queen was likely to be punished for committing a crime against God as well. That meant being hanged, cut open or burnt for the crime of **treason**.

Sometimes people commit crimes that are not about stealing or killing. At least, not to begin with. Their strong views cause them to commit crimes against the government or leaders of a country.

Such crimes can be a threat to a country's peace and security. Governments have often been quick to punish criminals that pose a threat to them. These may be:

- People who have tried to change the law but have ended up breaking it.
- People who have led protests against the government but have upset those with power.
- People who have given secrets to an enemy country or passed on government secrets.

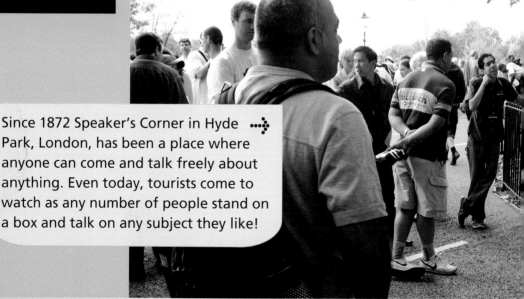

Since 1872 Speaker's Corner in Hyde Park, London, has been a place where anyone can come and talk freely about anything. Even today, tourists come to watch as any number of people stand on a box and talk on any subject they like!

*Word bank*    **human rights**   right of people to freedom of speech and being treated fairly & equally

## Freedom fighters

Through history people have fought against governments to try to change things for the better. Many people ended up in prison for 'disturbing the peace'. That often meant just speaking their views in public. The **freedom of speech** and **human rights** that many countries have today had to be fought for.

## Terror

Crimes against authority can be violent. Some criminals have felt so strongly that they have tried to kill leaders, the police or ordinary people. They set out to scare people into agreeing to their demands. Such **terrorists** have been at work all through history. In some places they are now more active than ever.

## The gunpowder plot

Guy Fawkes (below) and his gang of terrorists hated the British king and government so they tried to blow them up on 5th November, 1605. They failed and soldiers caught them. They were **tortured** before being put to death for treason. Their heads were stuck on poles and put on display. That was meant to stop others from having similar ideas!

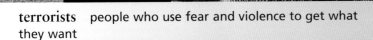

**terrorists**    people who use fear and violence to get what they want

In the UK in 1715 a new law called the Riot Act made it a crime for twelve people or more to meet and not break up if told to do so. If a crowd was "read the Riot Act", anyone could be arrested. That could lead to being transported across the world or even being hanged.

# Protests

Today people expect to be treated fairly in their work place. That was not so 200 years ago. Bosses could treat their workers badly. If anyone complained, they would be out of work and even poorer. It was a crime to go on strike or to encourage other workers to strike.

In 1833 in Dorset, UK, about 40 farm workers met in secret. They were worried about cuts in their wages. Their bosses **accused** them of planning a strike. The men were **arrested** and six of them were sent to Australia for seven years of **hard labour.**

Huge public protests to change the law followed. The men were finally brought home.

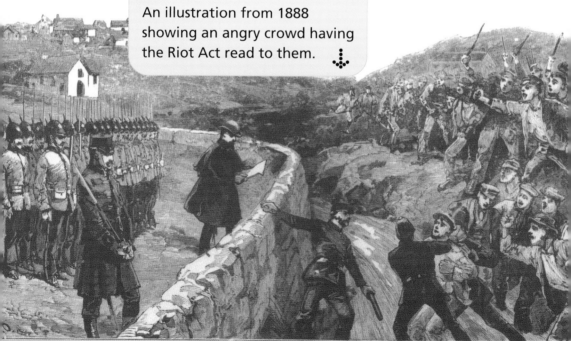

An illustration from 1888 showing an angry crowd having the Riot Act read to them.

*Word bank*    **hard labour**   tiring physical work

## Civil rights protests

Can you imagine a law that says "It all depends on what you look like as to whether you can have a seat on a bus?" Just over 50 years ago it was a crime for some people to go to some public places just because of how they looked. Black people in some states in the United States were banned from doing many things, like voting, simply because of their colour. Many people did not get a say in how their country was run.

In the 1960s there were many protests across the United States. By 1964 it became a crime to treat anyone differently because of "race, colour, or religion."

People gather for a civil rights protest in Washington, Alabama, 1963.

### All change on the buses

In 1955 a black woman in Alabama refused to obey the rule of giving up her bus seat to a white passenger. She was Rosa Parks (above) and she was arrested. Many black people then refused to use buses at all. Many protests followed until the rule to keep black and white people apart on buses was stopped a year later.

33

## Terror

Some criminals are prepared to kill many people – as well as themselves – to make their point.

When a massive bomb blew up the Federal Building in Oklahoma City, United States, in 1995, 168 people died. Americans were shocked to find this was not the work of a gang of terrorists. The killer was a 27 year old American called Timothy McVeigh. He hated the US government and chose to attack with violence. He was caught and sentenced to death.

In 2001 McVeigh was given a **lethal** injection in prison. He had caused the worst **terrorist** attack on American soil. Just three months after his death an even worse attack was to stun the world.

### The Brighton bomb

In 1984 terrorists tried to kill the UK prime minister and members of the government. They strongly disagreed with how Northern Ireland was being ruled. They planted a large bomb in the hotel where government members were staying. Although the leaders escaped, five people died and 34 were injured. Five men were sent to prison for the crime.

The Grand Hotel ⋯▸ in Brighton, after the terrorist bomb exploded in 1984.

*Word bank*   **Al-Qaeda**  terrorist organization behind the attacks on some countries

## September 11

In 2001 the world watched in horror as the World Trade Centre twin towers in New York were destroyed by two hijacked airliners. Another airliner crashed into the Pentagon building in Washington, D.C. A fourth plane crashed into a field in Pennsylvania after passengers fought back against the hijackers. The terrorist group **Al-Qaeda** admitted carrying out this crime that killed over 3,000 people.

In 1998, Bin Laden, the leader of Al Qaeda, told all his followers how he hated America. He hated what the American government was doing in Israel and other countries. He wanted Americans, their friends, and their way of life to be attacked.

The Oklahoma Federal Building after the attack in 1995.

### More attacks

A terrorist bomb in Bali (above) killed 202 people in October 2002. A year later four members of a terrorist group called Jemaah Islamiah were sentenced to death for this crime. In 2004 the same organization was thought to be behind a car bomb that killed people outside the Australian embassy in Jakarta.

# Solving crime

In 1784 in England, John Toms was convicted of murder because of a scrap of newspaper found stuck in a pistol at a crime scene. It exactly matched a piece of paper in his pocket. This was one of the first cases to match **evidence** from a murder weapon to a **suspect** to solve a crime.

The methods used to solve crimes over time have changed a lot, even in the last few years.

It was not until the 1750s that the first team of paid policemen began to tackle crime in London. They were called the Bow Street Runners. It was 1829 before a proper organized police force started. Other cities round the world followed several years later.

In 1835, a clever piece of detective work proved that tiny details at a crime scene can catch criminals. Henry Goddard, a London policeman, studied a mark on a bullet found in a murder victim. It matched marks in a suspect's gun. Case solved.

The study of fingerprints brought great progress to detective work.

*Word bank*    innocent   not guilty

## Fingerprints

The police discovered that everyone leaves behind fingerprints on what they touch. Each person's prints are different from other people's. This discovery led to changes in police work:

1880    Henry Faulds was a Scottish doctor in Tokyo. He said that fingerprints at the scene of a crime could identify the criminal. In one of the first uses of fingerprints to solve a crime, Faulds proved a suspect in a Tokyo **burglary** was **innocent**.

1903    New York State Prison first used fingerprints to identify criminals.

1905    Fingerprints were first used in the UK to convict a murderer.

1910    Fingerprints were first used in the US to convict a criminal.

*Catching killers red-handed*

In the early 1900s, Karl Landsteiner (below) of Austria discovered the four human blood groups (A, B, AB, and O). This was important for matching blood samples at crime scenes. Once it could be proved that blood found on a suspect was the victim's blood, detective work really took off.

## Crime scene clues

Over the last 100 years, detectives have made great progress in how they find clues at crime scenes. Scientists have made even more progress in how they examine these clues. As microscopes became more powerful to show tiny details left at a crime, the police became better at catching criminals.

Edmund Locard was once a policeman in Lyons in France. In 1910 he became a **professor** of **forensic** science. He set up the first police crime **laboratory** to study **evidence** from crime scenes. In 1920 he explained how all people leave tiny traces behind them wherever they go. This has led to many criminals being caught and proved **guilty**.

## Insect clues

When the police find a dead body they have to work out when, where, how and why the person died. From the 1960s insects became an important part of murder investigations. Scientists could work out the time of death from the age of insects living on the body.

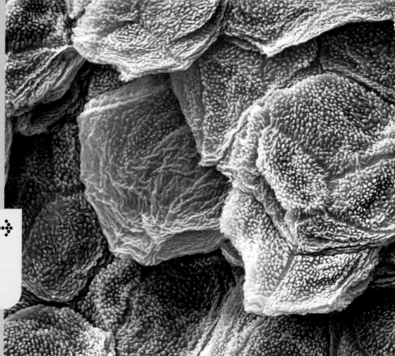

Human skin cells ⋯➤ can be seen clearly under a powerful microscope.

*Word bank*  laboratory  special room fitted out for scientific research

## New science

In the last 50 years scientists have developed ways to study tiny specks of dust, pollen, hair, blood and **fibres**. They can often tell today not just if a **suspect** was at the scene of a crime but exactly where – and sometimes when. Criminals not only leave tiny traces of themselves behind but they also pick up little specks of material from a scene.

From the 1950s scientists could study blood stains under a microscope and tell if they came from a man or a woman. In another 30 years they could match specks of blood and tell exactly who they came from. That was bad news for murderers!

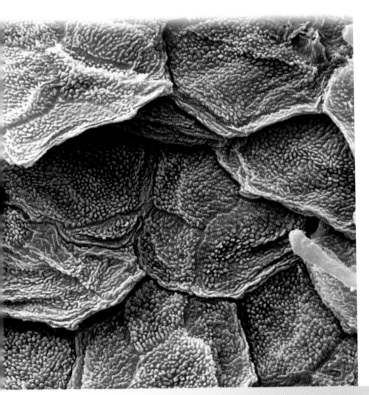

**post-mortem**   examination of a dead body to find the cause of death
**professor**   someone who has studied a subject to a very high level

## Breakthrough

In the last 20 years, two great developments changed crime-solving forever.

### Proof

A teenage boy was arrested for killing a girl in the UK in 1983. The police called in Dr Jeffreys who had been working on DNA testing. He proved the boy was not the killer at all. Dr Jeffreys said: "I have no doubt that the **suspect** would have been found guilty had it not been for DNA **evidence**."

### 1. The discovery of **DNA**

DNA is a chemical inside each of our cells. It is like a special code locked in our **genes**. Every person's DNA is different. It can be found in blood, hair, body fluids or cells. It was Alec Jeffreys, a UK scientist, who developed DNA tests in 1984. It was first used to solve a crime two years later.

### 2. Computers

Databases can now store, sort, check and match huge amounts of information. The police can quickly search millions of records for a criminal's DNA or fingerprints. Detective work will never be the same again!

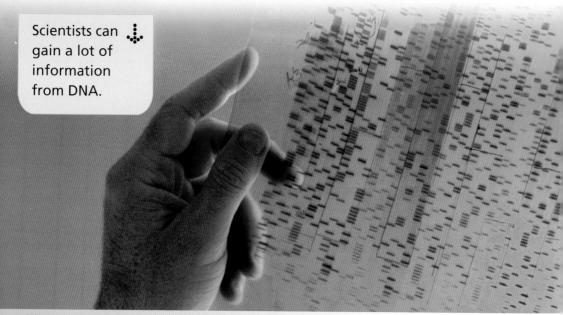

Scientists can gain a lot of information from DNA.

**DNA** special code in each person's genes that makes them individual

## Solving mysteries

Many unsolved crimes from the past have been solved today by using modern DNA tests. Blood samples that were kept from crimes of years ago have since led to **arrests**. Even dead criminals have been found **guilty**! By taking DNA from bones in graves, the police have been able to prove if a dead person was a killer or not.

All convicted criminals today have to give a DNA sample. This information is kept on computer records. It may only be a matter of time before everyone's DNA information is kept on police records. Crimes could soon be solved at the press of a button!

### Case re-opened

Helena Greenwood was found strangled to death in her San Diego home in 1985. Police suspected David Frediani of the crime but there was no evidence. That was until 2000 when the case was re-opened. Skin particles under Helena's fingernails were proved to match Frediani's DNA. Case solved. He was convicted at last.

Just a small amount of DNA on a swab is all police scientists need to find vital clues.

# And finally...

## Guess what...

- Today US police **arrest** about 3,000 people per day.
- Every day 400 purses get snatched and 1,000 people are victims of pick pockets in America. The average theft is US$250.
- US$20,000 per day is stolen from vending machines in the United States.

Many people today say, "Crime has never been as bad as it is now."

By looking back at the painful history of crime, it is easy to see that this is not always true! Today more crimes get reported and appear on the news so it SEEMS like crime is worse. We tend to hear all about the bad news and not about all the crime that is stopped or solved. In fact, over the last 50 years, crime rates in many countries have gone down. As living standards, food, health and wages improve, the levels of some crimes fall.

···> Crime happens in the streets every day.

## Always changing

Over time different crimes have tended to rise and fall for many reasons. Some of those reasons have been:

- Growing towns – more people crowded together often cause more crime.
- The widening gap between the rich and the poor can make some people lose hope and turn to crime.
- The state of the police and prisons affect the crime rate. The better these are at preventing and solving crime, the less crime there will be.

It only remains to be seen how some of the causes of crime will change in the future. Will crime still be as painful as in its often grisly past?

### The good old days?

You may think we have tough laws today. Some of the old records for England show crimes that no longer exist:

- Robert Smith – fined for refusing to bury a dead pig – 1494
- Jas Hartas – fined for drying oats on a Sunday – 1576
- Four men fined for selling over-priced candles – 1577.

How times and crimes have changed!

Any clues how crime will change in the next 100 years?

# Find out more

## Around the world...

- South Africa has the most gun murders per head of population.

- Two-thirds of the world's executions occur in China.

- Two-thirds of the world's kidnappings occur in Colombia, where the average criminal sentence length is 137 years.
- Around 1 in 3 Australians are victims of crime.
- 0.7% of Americans are currently in prison.

## Books

*Behind the Scenes: Solving a Crime*, Peter Mellet (Heinemann Library, 1999)

*Forensic Files: Investigating Thefts & Heists*, Alex Woolf (Heinemann Library, 2004)

*Life in Prison*, Stanley Williams (SeaStar Books, 2001)

*True Crime: Cops and Robbers*, John Townsend (Raintree, 2005)

## Using the Internet

Explore the Internet to find out more about crime through time. You can use a search engine, such as www.yahooligans.com, and type in keywords such as:

- Amnesty International
- criminal
- highwaymen.

## Search tips

There are billions of pages on the Internet so it can be difficult to find exactly what you are looking for.

These search tips will help you find websites more quickly:

- Know exactly what you want to find out about first.
- Use two to six keywords in a search, putting the most important words first.
- Be precise. Only use names of people, places, or things.

# Crime Through Time

| | | |
|---|---|---|
| 1215 | England | Writing of the Magna Carta (Law of the land). |
| 1253 | England | Parish constables start patrolling some areas, being paid by local residents. |
| 1475 | England | **Invention** of the muzzle-loading musket. |
| 1539 | England | First criminal court established at Old Bailey. |
| 1718 | England | Machine gun invented by James Puckle. |
| 1789 | United States | Constitution (Law) **ratified**. |
| 1829 | UK | Sir Robert Peel begins a proper police force with 1,000 uniformed police officers, based at Scotland Yard, London. |
| 1830 | United States | First revolver made by Samuel Colt. |
| 1833 | United States | First paid police force in the United States, based in Philadelphia. |
| 1868 | UK | Last public hanging in Britain. |
| 1870 | United States | Creation of Department of Justice. |
| 1878 | UK | Creation of Criminal Investigation Department. |
| 1935 | United States | Bureau of Investigations becomes the Federal Bureau of Investigations (FBI). |
| 1936 | United States | Last public hanging in the United States. |
| 1987 | UK | First use of DNA typing in solving crimes. |

# Glossary

**accused** charged with committing a crime

**Al-Qaeda** terrorist organization behind the attacks on some countries

**arrested** taken in for questioning about a crime

**authority** people in charge such as the government of a country

**black market** illegal trade that is against government controls

**branded** marked with a red hot iron tool

**burglar** someone who breaks into a building or house to steal, especially at night

**confess** own up to doing something wrong

**convicted** proved to be guilty

**criminal** person who has committed a crime

**customs** office at borders of countries where taxes are paid on imports or exports

**cyber crime** anything illegal using computers

**death penalty** being put to death as a punishment for a crime

**DNA** special code in each person's genes that makes them individual

**evidence** material presented to a court to help find the truth in a crime

**export** goods sent to another country to sell

**FBI** United State's Federal Bureau of Investigation, which investigates serious crime

**fibres** tiny threads

**flintlock musket** gun with a flint making a spark to fire the gunpowder

**forensic** detailed scientific study to help solve crimes

**fraud** cheating people out of money by deceiving them in some way

**freedom of speech** being able to speak freely about ideas and beliefs in public

**gallows** wooden frame from which criminals were hanged

**gene** the set of instructions inside our cells

**guilty** having done wrong

**hard labour** tiring physical work

**homicide** killing of one human being by another

**human rights** right of people to freedom of speech and being treated fairly and equally

**identity theft** stealing people's personal details and pretending to be them

**illegal** against the law

**impulse** sudden idea to do something

**innocent** not guilty

**invent** make or discover something for the first time

**laboratory** special room fitted out for scientific research

**larceny** crime of carrying away someone's personal property deliberately

**lethal** dangerous and deadly

**Middle Ages** period of European history from about 800 to about 1500

**offence** breaking of the law

**ordeal** painful test

**outlaws** criminals who lived "outside the law"

**pharaoh** ruler of ancient Egypt

**piracy** robbery on the high seas

**poaching** stealing animals from private land

**pope** head of the Roman Catholic church

**post-mortem** examination of a dead body to find the cause of death

**professor** someone who has studied a subject to a very high level

**ratified** be made official

**revenge** get even for a wrong done

**sacred** holy and worthy of respect

**scold** someone who keeps complaining and nagging

**slum** crowded and run-down part of a town

**smallpox** deadly fever and rash caused by a virus

**suspect** someone who is thought to be guilty of a crime

**tavern** "ale house" where alcoholic drinks are sold and drunk

**tax** charge set by government to pay for running the country

**terrorism** use of terror to achieve a goal

**terrorists** people who use fear and violence to get what they want

**torture** causing someone great pain especially to punish or to obtain a confession

**treason** crime of trying to overthrow the government or authority

**vandalism** damaging property on purpose

# Index

# Titles in the *A Painful History Of Crime* series include:

Hardback         1 844 21391 9

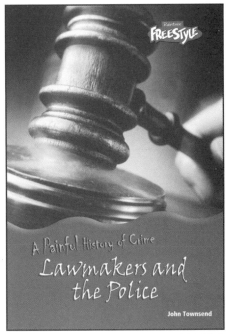

Hardback         1 844 21390 0

Hardback         1 844 21389 7

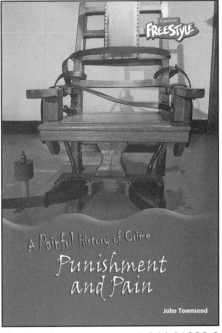

Hardback         1 844 21388 9

Find out about other titles on our website www.raintreepublishers.co.uk